Sublimation

Sublimation

A Collection of Poems

STUTI ASHOK GUPTA

PARTRIDGE
A Penguin Random House Company

To order additional copies of this book, contact
Partridge India
000 800 10062 62
orders.india@partridgepublishing.com

www.partridgepublishing.com/india

Contents

I will kill
Not with weapons
But with poetry.

I will kill
Without guns
But with words.

Like every poet,
I want to give people
More than one death –
No pain, no bloodshed.

I want to give people heartache
Without breakups and betrayal.
I want to give people dreams
Without sleep
Or fear that they won't come true.

Introduction

When I sat down to write the introduction, I thought, "Let's refer some other works!" I saw the books of Kamala Das, Rabindranath Tagore, Rumi, Gulzar and a few others. One thing common with all of them was that the introduction was written by someone else. It's true that such great authors do not require an introduction. "But that's not fair," I whispered in my head – I am required to give an introduction.

There must be thousands of books that are being published in the world and I could be adding just one more to the shelves labelled "Poems" in libraries and bookstores that people hardly visit in this digital age.

This book is an honest attempt to touch your heart. We all go through something in our lives, fighting it in our own heroic ways. God has designed our lives like a jigsaw, with the pieces dispersed everywhere. Life is a process of bringing all the pieces together and death is the ultimate finish line. It isn't necessary that you make sense of this jigsaw.

In Greek tragedy, Aristotle introduced the concept of "hamartia" which means "a tragic flaw"—a shortcoming in the hero. We are all consumed in our own tragedies, trying to identify the true hamartia. This collection of poems talks about my hamartia, which you—as the reader—might be able to relate to in some way or the other.

The book starts with a series of love poems and delves deeper into the idea of pain. We wander in pain to fill a void: a chronic emptiness that hits us every night, no matter where we are. From what I have observed, we like to be in control of our lives to not turn hysterical and to be able to predict this fortuitous life. We choose loneliness and isolation to protect ourselves from the pain that follows overwhelming connections.

The fourth chapter of the book focuses on the nuances of pain that accompany loss—that phase of life which is monotonous and fixed in schedules and appointments. What do you feel when you stop feeling the pain? A mother mourning her child's death; a lover longing for his beloved... What do they feel once the pain stops? They begin to question everything that happens around them.

We interrogate the truth behind smiling faces and empathize with black cats. We get agitated by small talk. The observation of the outside world becomes a question mark, which eventually turns inward. The fifth chapter of the book questions our existence. It talks about grocery lists, about the idea of a home, about the poems that die in a poet's mind and about the phony WhatsApp conversations that end with blue tick marks and no replies. It also explores the significance of our lives in absolute relativity to the countless number of galaxies in the universe.

The book closes in admiration for nature and how it evokes in us the subtleties of love, longing, parting and pain.

Acknowledgement

My mother, Chandrakanta Gupta, has been a constant support and has pushed me to do this since the day I told her I wanted to publish. My father, Ashok Gupta, who I get my writing skills and witty humour from, has always been an inspiration. Agnim, my brother (and my toughest critic), has always challenged me to achieve more than I think I can. I am grateful to my family for being there.

I am also grateful to Partridge India, my publishing services associates Gemma Ramos and Mary Oxley for their patience; my book editor Kaushal LS and my book's cover designer Pranita Kocharekar (@untilnexttime_cards).

Thanks to all my colleagues and friends – Hina Jain, Maitraiye Sharma, Ishani Badyal, Rubaina Kunder, Aakansha Singhal, Divisha Rastogi, Shatanik Singh, Laharee Mitra, Astik Gupta, Niveshi Jain, Shubham Singh and Akshay Vaid. I would also like to extend my gratitude to everyone who took their precious time to help me even though I might not be able to mention all the names here. I'm thankful for the brilliant reactions I received at the news that I was going to publish – I felt truly loved.

I am grateful for the little contributions from each of you – from reading my poems, to talking things over, to appreciating, to honest criticisms and discussions. I beg the forgiveness of all those who have been there for me and whose names I have failed to mention.

बागर्था विव संपृक्तौ बागर्था प्रतिपत्तये ।
जगत: पतिरौ बन्दे पार्वती परमेश्वरौ ॥

All the Love

If He Watches Cartoons With You

If he watches cartoons with you
And calls you a superhero name or two,
Never let him go.
If he buys you an ice cream but eats most of it on his own
And gives you roses in spite of the prickly thorns,
Never let him go.

If he comes all the way to the airport
But hopes that you miss your flight
And gets anxious like a baby
When you are out of his sight,
Never let him go.
If he cooks for you, his favourite dish
And the right music, he does not miss,
Never let him go.

If he crosses his fingers every time he asks you out
And kisses you on the cheek when you pout,
Never let him go.
Even after saying he's leaving, he stays
And messes up your hair as he plays,
Never let him go.

If he gets you books that challenge your beliefs
And laughs at your joy and weeps when you grieve
Never let him go.
If he understands the pain of losing a pet

And takes a walk with you on a cold, foggy night,
Never let him go.

If people think you're siblings for the way you fight
And talk about God and the things you believe in some
    nights,
Never let him go.
If you're thinking of someone as you read this poem,
Chances are he's already gone
Or he was never there in the first place.

Look around.
Look how the birds chirp at the first rays of sun
And how the moon shines at night.
He could be looking at the same too,
Maybe in a different time zone.
Maybe in a different country.
Thinking in a different language
Of you, without knowing you –
Like you are, without knowing him.

Pastel Crayons

I do care about
Who you are,
Where you are from and
How much air you take in one breath;
How many butterflies do you
Like on your plate at once?
How many hearts have you
Broken with those shiny shoes?
Have you ever been in love?

I do care
If you've had death wishes,
About your day dreams
And your nightmares
And if your heart is kind enough
To take the shattered pieces of mine
And make it one.

I do care about
When you wake up
And when you sleep
And who you think of
Every time you weep;
How deep is your unconscious
And the words
You will never speak?

Will you tell me about
All the pastel crayons
That were sacrificed to
Make you so colourful?

I do care
About you.
You should let me.
Will you let me?

Jet Lag

Even though
Your days and your nights
Are different
From my days and my nights,
Even though
Your wrongs are my rights,
My wrongs: your rights,
We both know
How our hands jitter
And our feet shuffle
When we have to wait
In a long queue:
Impatience is nothing new
For me and for you.

But you're a fool, remember?
For shaking up my grandiosity
Of being the only one.
You're a fool
For being the hopeless romantic
That you are.

Remember that time you emptied
The last of the tobacco
From your self-made cigar

As you told me
About the melting snow
And the dew that's formed?

But it's good that we are
In two different time zones
'Cause we never get to say
Goodnight to each other,
And that serves us right.

Raw Mangoes

As I was eating
Raw mangoes
All by myself,
I realised:
Some things shouldn't be done alone.

I went back
To struggling with my curiosity…
To know what went wrong.

Was it that
I didn't give you the reaction you expected
When you made me watch
Your favourite song's video?
The one you were so excited about?

Or is it that my hair is all messy
And you always look personable?
Or the fact my lips are like those of a chain smoker
While yours are pink like an infant's?

Was it that I laughed
When you called yourself an asshole?
Did you want me
To tell you that you're not?

Or when you said,
"I love you!"
With that thing you do with your eyes
And I called you a liar?

Was it that I couldn't finish
That spicy wrap by myself

And you had to eat
The rest of it too?

But, baby,
Some things can't be done alone.

At the Mention of Your Name

You live within me
Like I have two souls.

I sigh, I cry,
With the best of me, I try
To keep you inside.
But a smile shines through my eyes
At the mention of your name
Without anyone's notice
Every once in a while.

You come out like a gust of wind,
Whisking all the sighs away
And all my quiet goes to waste.
It's impossible to hide you within
At the mention of your name.

If someone peers into me,
They'd see all of you.

Valentine

I'm a big fan
Of 2:41 AM conversations
And little yellow notes
Scribbled on with the black ink
That remains on the tip
Of his index finger
As it does on mine
All day long –
Lingering on every piece of work.

Red roses, chocolate tarts
And soft toys that
Constantly fail to remind us
Of childhood innocence
Cease to exist –
Forgotten, in a dark corner.

Slow dancing, addictive perfumes,
Fairy lights, lamps and candle-lit dinners,
Late night movie marathons
And the arguments that follow,
And the cuddles and kisses,
Calling each other
Mister and missus;
'Cause I'm a big fan
Of fancy weddings

And stories of love and parting,
Big shiny diamond rings.

Tubs of ice cream,
Airports and railway stations,
Hand-in-hand under the moon,
Being carefree of what I wear,
And bad video quality
Skype calls with messy hair,
Trying to reach out,
Figuring out
What the other person is trying to say.

Singing *Bohemian Rhapsody* together,
Breathing in harmony,
Sceptical laughter,
Sarcastic comments
But sincere tears
And never too tired to hear,
"I love you,
I want to be with you."
Of course, those honest prayers,
Talking about how it would be like
When we turn 40 or 55.

I'm a big fan of all that
But all of it –
Forever out of reach.

Ruminate

I keep looking...
Looking for him
On the busy streets,
At the airport,
Up in the clouds,
In the water.

I keep looking...
Looking for him
Inside the cars
Ahead of me,
Behind, as I walk
Or as I drive.

I keep looking…
Looking for him
In the trains,
In the flights,
In the movie halls and
In the corridors
Where nothingness
Seems to thrive.

I keep looking...
Looking for him
On theatre stages
And on the TV.

Sometimes, I just imagine him
Walking towards me
From nowhere –
Getting closer and closer.
I imagine him
Doing that thing
With his eyes and lower lip.

I see him in my dreams...
I weave my day dreams
Such that I have him, all of him.
I sense him
In the silence of the ghost stories.
I wish it was him
Sitting at the corner table
In that random coffee shop,
Sipping his Americano
As I enjoy my green apple.

I often find myself saying
"Look! That stranger's hair
Is just like his!"
I keep looking for him everywhere.

As Long as You Can

As much as I want to curl up
In your shade,
You push me towards growth.
But don't you know, darling,
That as my petals uncurl
And I bloom in the dark,
I'll be put into a garland
And then on a stone.

Let me be a bud forever
In your shade and in your softness –
If ever I must bloom,
Darling, not now...

Keep me as close as you can
For as long as you can.

Keep Me

Little bits of ash, flying
Little bit of sweet kindness
Got you here now, love.
So if you call me and
Ask me to fight tonight,
I will let you win, love.

You're too fervent.
I'm a ball of fire, too –
We will burn the city down
One day, love.

But until then,
Keep calling me, baby.
Keep me in your
Frequently dialled.
Keep me in your memory,
In your daydreams, love.

Run Out

I might run out of
Words when we talk
I might run out of
Hugs as we walk

I might run out of stories of tell
I might run out of reasons to yell
That I have held for years, inside.

And, baby, I might run out of poetry too
But never love.
I will never run out of love.

On the Roads

Husky voice.
Dusky skin.
Tiny eyes.
And a wide smile
That could confine
All of my madness
In between those teeth.
If I ever find him
At a random metro station
Or a subway,
I would ask him
To sing that song
That had me awestruck
The first time.
And every time after
I'd tell him,
"On the road, now you'd see,
Maybe all of me,
Maybe all of me."

I Love You

Those three words,
A gulp in his throat.
My heart aches, it erodes
When he says, "I love you."

His eyes turn away
As mine chases his that way
When he says, "I love you."

A reflex of words, I swear, "Oh!"
Not planned, hope he does know
When he says, "I love you."

So unplanned
Awaited, so in demand
When he says, "I love you."

The wind of love turns into a hurricane,
Clouds burst, eyes rain
When he says, "I love you."

That moment I look for all the time,
It is unjustified: sure, a crime
When he says, "I love you."

I forget everything I want to say.
My wax of strength begins to melt.
Impulsive that I am,
I tell him I love him too
When he says, "I love you"

Release

Sometimes I wish I could stop.
I could stop waiting
'Cause waiting gives me hope.
Sometimes I wish someone could
Cast a magic spell
To make me drift like the clouds,
Moving on.
Sometimes, I wish I do not feel at all
'Cause when I do,
I only feel the space
In distance
In time
In life
In friends
In the food that we eat every day
In the clothes
On the roads that we walk every day
In colours
In the weather
In the birds we watch
In the stars we count
We are not just separated by distance
We are separated by an entire lifetime
While you have released me,
I am learning to release you.

Use You

I would use you
Like a fire extinguisher
But only when the fire
Within me is
Burning me and everything around.

I would use you
Like a dance move
That I thoroughly know
On stage,
One that fits in every bar,
Every beat,
When I miss the one I learnt.

I would use you
Like the veto power
When the case seems so unfair
That I can't take it anymore.
Like the expensive perfume
For my special dates.

I would use you
Like the favourite outfit
And also the last piece
Of clothing,

When I don't know what
Else I could cover
My vulnerabilities with.

I would use you
Like the last call
Before I leap to death:
My own suicide helpline.
Like the song I listen to
When I'm too low
And when the sadness hits.
And until then, never again.

I would use you
Like the last prayer
To God, when I know
Nothing feels right.

I would use you
Like party poppers
To make my birthday
A little more special.

I would use you
In pain, in failure
In heart aches and
Moments of blur.

Most of all
I would make sure
I remain happy
Most often.

You're my need
Any day, any night.
I cannot use you
Too much;
Indeed my plight.

Air

I want to be wherever you are.
I want to be the air you breathe.
Never leave you, nor choke you.
Breathe me in
When you are tensed.
Breathe me out, yawning like a child,
Carelessly demanding for sleep.

Open all your windows and doors
And watch me dance my madness for you
And then close them in the middle of the night
As I keep your feet cold and hands warm.
I will kiss you with the fragrance.

Not like light nor shade,
Not like the sun and the moon,
They all leave.
Like air,
I want to be present everywhere
Where it is pitch dark
I want to be wherever you are.

When I Met You

When I met you
Last November,
I remember
There was a rhythm
That your pulse created
When my ear
Was beside your neck.
I remember
The rhythm that
Your heart made
When I put my head
On your chest.

That sounded like
Love.

Of Harmony & Chaos

I sensed my heartbeat and his too,
Sometimes in harmony
Creating a symphony
In unison,
Sometimes in utter chaos.

Even in the dead of night, our chests
Rhythmically rose and fell
And rose and fell
And our breaths tuned into the sound
That surrounded the night.

My mind was racing:
A million words all at once
But my body was eased onto his,
Curled into a safe house.

Does he know how wonderful his touch feels to me?
I'd leave all the rivers, mountains and scenery,
For the feeling of fitting so perfectly next to him
But for now darling, your ignorance is my bliss –
I'll lay by you now and forever in this memory.

All the branches don't point to the same part of the sky,
But what do I do when I have to choose one side?
You make the branches merge into one,

Touching my feet.
I get everything I want, at once and for all.

Even time I sit alone,
I feel the brush of your fingers against my arm.
It's a phantom memory
But your memories somehow smell sweeter than you.

I can sense an invisible layer of rich colours
On my skin even now.
And the invisible never fades.

Only if it were poetry, it would have lines –
My love is a circle,
Where I have been taking rounds all these years.
And circles never end.

(Written with Laharee Mitra)

Voids

You know, those orange-ish white voids
In between the blue floating clouds:
They make me wish...
Wish you were watching me from above.
Do you imagine
Me applying *kajal*?
'Cause I imagine you
Fixing your hair.
Every day I wish religiously
That you were next to me,
Laughing at my poetry.

As I watch the voids
Get filled,
The blue turns to grey –
It's getting gloomy,
Sand is all I see.
Under the old palm tree,
The light dims as I cease to feel.
I don't mind this darkness,
I don't mind this feeling of being lost
Where I can be with you
And you, with me.

The Best Therapy

You have been
The best therapy
For my healing heart.
Where are you now?

Flashbacks of memories
From my previous life
Are haunting me at night.

Come back,
Before I relapse
All over again,
Just like I always do.

My Compulsions

All day
In vacuum I loiter
Till you rush in
Like air at night.

All day
In thirst I wander
Till you flood in
Like water at night.

All day
In hunger I surrender
Till you show up
Like food delivery at midnight.

For my heart,
For my impulsion –
Like a crest and its trough,
Like ups and downs,
You play around
With my obsessions,
With my compulsions.

Love Is a Heavy Word

Love is a heavy word.
So I pretend to hold it
Loosely like a flower
Tucked carelessly
In the loose plait
Of a woman
Too scared to
Fall in love.
But when nobody's
Around, I hold it
As tight as I can
Like a pillow
That won't hug
Me back.

The Moon and the Ocean

To and fro,
The eyes keep searching
To calm
Their weariness.
The blackness under them
Is not smudged mascara,
But soot
From the burning heart.
It's only when the eyes
Have rested enough, that lips
Will rest on the lips,
Hands will rest on the waist,
Moving along the curves.
And the clouds like hands
Will cover the eyes
Of the moon,
So it doesn't mourn,
For its distance
From the ocean
When we meet,
So the stars
Don't envy
The twinkle in our eyes.

Black Hole

His smile
Shows her the Milky Way
Of a universe she knows not of;
In his eyes,
She can see his story
Like a screening
In a planetarium.

He smirks
And constellations merge,
Her laughter
Is the music of a falling star
That puts him to sleep.
Her sobs
Causes eclipses.

Their kisses
Make the sun burn brighter.
Eventually, everything is consumed
By the fire of their unison,
Turning it all into
An absolute black hole.

Eyes and Lips

When the lips smile,
The corner of the eyes wrinkle
Just like the butterflies in my stomach
When I look at his smile.

When the lips
Remember God
With its words,
Eyes close
In harmony and peace.

When the lips
Cheat on the eyes
With another,
Lips meet,
Eyes shut; indifferent –
In denial.

It's the eyes that turn red
As the lips reflect anger
But it's the eyes that weep
As lips part from lips.

I want a love like
The lips and the eyes,
Where the love never dies.

Voice

I swear to God
And all the beautiful things I've seen,
There's nothing like your voice.
It's so deep,
I could dive into it,
Float around,
Traverse and explore
The little starfish and plankton
But I know
You hide your Bermuda Triangle
That makes me feel like
There is no coming back
From where I sink.
I sink in,
Deeper and deeper
But I'm afraid that I'll find
A hundred hearts just like mine
Alive yet drowning,
Waiting for help.

Yellow Dress

I'll call this feeling
A yellow dress,
Bright and happy
For a fine, sunny day.

Too risky
To let me be
Carefree;
For I'm afraid
A drop of ketchup
Will leave a stain on it,
Leaving me guilty
For tainting my heart.

But you add colour
To my dress
But I'm scared
It might just fade;
The brightest yellow
Might turn just turn mellow.

Love Note

Don't discard me
Because I look like
Someone else's
Abandoned love letter.
Does it matter?

Keep me in your
Antique box,
Keep me in your
Memories.
Take it,
Unfold it
Read word-for-word.
Because chances are
You might find something...
Something you wanted to say
For years, to someone.

Sometimes, the words didn't come out right.
Sometimes, the woman
Didn't arrive on time.

Dreams

Stop visiting me in my dreams,
I'm at my weakest there.
In the middle of it,
When I feel a little cold,
I see you climb down from somewhere
So that you could lie down next to me.

Your flaming heart
Blisters my soul every night.
Against my flow, you're the downstream,
White noise to my screams.
Love, stop coming into my dreams.

Unknown Playlist

There's an acoustic guitar
Playing along
To that song in a playlist
I never made
But recently found.
I am unsure,
So I go round and round
About what it's trying to say
Through each and every song.
It's sweet, it's absurd.
I have never heard it before, I'm sure.
I'm too lost in this symphony –
I hope you know,
I am not talking about
The song alone.

She's a Happy Song

Lost track of years
But I remember moments
Of love and anger,
Exploring and exposing
Our hearts, naked.

Late night conversations
That go on till the break of dawn
With the girl who lets me cry.
She wears her smile
As if she is showing it off,
Dancing, like a stone skipping on water
Before it sinks completely,
Causing ripples.

Hysteria is the definition
Of her laughter
And man!
When she hugs me
She gives me
The feeling of being loved.

Each time she looks at me
From the corner of the room,
Every time I meet her gaze,

I run into myself somehow.
I don't know how.
I swear, I don't know how.

She can read a sad poem
That I wrote at 3:00 AM.
Yet, she manages to remain
A happy song, somehow.
I don't know how.
I so wonder how.

Impulsive Lover

An intense need
To cuddle
To be around someone
To have a conversation
And cut off the silence
To act out of impatience
To react impulsively
Saying your thoughts out loud
Walking away from a tense situation

To express a lot
To shut yourself up
When you don't receive
What you deserve
To be needy,
To get greedy
Of attention.

Things of short-lived pleasure
Are harmful in the long run
And things that upset you,
Challenge you, shake you up,
Those are the ones that show their
Beautiful colours in the larger picture.

Imagine water colours:
Too much water
Or too much colour,
Both can spoil the painting;
What matters is the wisdom
To choose the right mix.

Change is inevitable
And so is suffering.

If someone likes you,
Loves you
Or wants to be around you,
They always find a way.
Dear girls,
And their respective girlfriends,
Stop assessing
That strange looks and smirks
From a guy are signs
That he is attracted to you.

A guy who sincerely wants to have you
Won't play hard to get.

Yours,
An impulsive lover.

Muse

Be my muse tonight
And all the nights
From dawn to dusk
And round the clock.

Be my insomnia
When I struggle
To fall asleep.

Be my unconscious
When I sink
Into oblivion.

Be the voice
I wake up to
And sleep to.

Be the arms
That hold me,
That pull me closer.

Be my impatience
That is curious and wild.

Be my muse tonight.
Darling, be my muse
Tonight.

Mostly French

He told her he wouldn't sleep all night long
When she was around.
He exhaled circles of smoke,
She inhaled it like the only truth
That came out of his mouth –
Like poison that might kill her one day.

Smoking kills, the box read.
"What doesn't kill?"
He intervened.

He told her he would stay up all night, kissing
And talking and losing himself again and again.
He liked the way she erupted like little volcanoes
Like the fizz of beer from a can.
She had kissed before, lain next to men before
And every time she woke up in the morning,
The space next to her was always empty,
Her fingers left empty.

They spoke in languages they couldn't fathom
In each other's mouths,
Mostly French.

He stayed, fitting perfectly into her curves
Of loneliness and insecurities.
Sleep never parted them –
It was as if she was always awake.

All the Pain

When You Left

When you left,
I felt like a kite
Stuck in a branch,
For years.

Torn here, torn there.
But at the heart,
It all seemed fine.

When you left
I felt unhinged,
Unleashed,
Afraid: too scared
For my freedom
And not knowing where to go.

When you left
I found a hole in my parachute
And I was falling.
I saw hands
Trying to grasp mine
But I was just
Throwing my hands in the air
Like an infant,
Unaware of gravity.

I managed to not
Land on my face
On the hard ground.
I did not make a sound.

When you left,
I felt lost and purposeless
The world seemed too crowded
All of a sudden,
Tall men and women.
And I couldn't have
One more look at you,
Everything looked
Unfamiliar and new.

When you left,
I did feel
Very lonely.
When you left,
I couldn't see anything at all.
When you left,
I didn't know
Where else to go,
Where else to go.

The Last Layer of Petals

Saw you in my dream
Last night –
You were blooming like
The last layer of petals
Of a rose.

Your chest
And my back,
Your legs
Tangled in mine.
While my body
Was curled up,
My heart was unfolding
In your arms, gently
Like a tiny bud
That hardly ever thought
Would open her eyes.

It was hard at first
But you made the world
Look like a safe place
Once again.
After the last time,
When I was plucked
By a lover
Like I was the one
But carelessly and callously left,

Forgotten on
A bench at a lovers' park.
It stained a woman's heart
With contagious crimson marks
On her favourite sweater.

And now all the places
She goes,
Those stains follow
While I remain,
That crushed, forgotten bud.

Last night,
In my dream,
As you brushed
Against me,
You brought me
Closest to this reality.

A Sea of My Own

Waves crash against the shore,
Getting harder and stronger
Than the ones before.
There is no moon light
But the white beams
At the fish stalls
That make my shadow
Fall on the sand,
Gently caressing
These indecisive waves
That come and go
Just like you.

There's nothing new,
About this feeling
Of striving to hold a hand.
I struggle to drench
Myself in your saltiness
To enter your world of immense love
While all I'm left with is
Sandy slippers and sticky feet.

Dry, itchy lenses
That blur my vision
And a feeling of paranoia,
Of being naive.

While I find the whole world
Yearning to fill
Their little voids
Through your humongous existence,
Sharing and struggling,
When will I ever have
A little sea of my own?

To Look At, To Come Back To

In some faraway land
Or space,
There is an ember that I see.
Smoke all over the sky,
Spreading its wings, far and wide.
How much further does it want to fly?

The waves crash against the shore
Are they howling in anger or joy?
Who knows?
I stand here
All by myself,
Wishing I had a shore too
To look at,
To come back to, to yearn for,
To sleep in the arms of –
After a long journey
From one land to another.

Sometimes I wonder,
If they are all stars,
What is so special about the sun?
He thinks the world revolves around him.
And I don't find an answer –
I never do.

There are little silhouettes
Blocking my vision
But the wind in my hair
Consoles me compassionately.

The wind knows it all.
So I ask,
"Am I just one of the many shores?
One of the many that the sea plays its games with?"

Unchaining

Tidily,
I unchain myself
From him.
I remove all the bangles
Of memories,
Unhook the earrings
And the nose pin,
Cleanse every inch of
Make up,
All the kisses,
All the hugs.
Undress my body
Of his love.
As I begin to shiver
From this cold wind,
I look for another
Sheet to cover
My naked heart –
Some are already
Dirty with others' makeup,
Some are taken
And the rest torn & destroyed.

I find a mirror:
I look at the reflection
Of a woman,
Bright colours –

Stuti Ashok Gupta

Yellow and pink.
It is me, dressed again
In tenderness;
Confused as I am,
Looking for the best
Jewellery to match it with
This time.

Once I have
Felt the softness of
A cloth, I have known
The beauty of the dazzling jewellery
And the jittery feeling in my stomach –
I cannot forget it
I cannot disown it
I cannot unlearn it.

Cracks

Cracks are good.
Good on the walls,
Letting the sun shine through,
Offering warmth on
A dreary, cold day.

Cracks are good.
Good on the skin
Letting life recite
Stories – both awful and delightful

And the heart?
It cracks because of gravity,
That's the beauty of it.
Have you ever wondered?
Why it's called
"Falling in love?"

Crawling

You've choked me
With this sadness.

You've left me in this position
Where I have cavities,
But you are
An awful temptation.

I wish I could give up
But you've given me these
Weird memories
That crawl into my mind
While I try to fall asleep.

The storm outside is terrible
Just like your silence.
These rains don't drench me anymore,
They only leave me feeling cold and dry.

Come, rush in,
Don't leave me hollow.

4:37 AM

Lights are shining at a distance
And my scalded lips
From this cigarette
Hurt much more this time
Without his lips to brush against mine.

Was it my fault
That his life has been a mess?
Was it reason enough
To mess with mine?

Our lives, like dominos.
Music playing in the background...
The Corrs, I assume,
Telling me,
"Everybody hurts, sometimes."

My hand and legs, shivering,
Too numb to move.
Someone is knocking at the door.
The wind wants to come in.
It's too late,
I don't know
If I should let it in.
It is 4:37 AM,
Never a good time
For a love confession,

To send a mail
Full of aggression.
It's never a good time
To fall asleep,
Especially when I am lonely.

All the windows are shut,
The mosquito repellent being
The only presence in the room.

Through which hole will
The closure I long for enter?

Dig in, fill in
This true void.
Sigh.

Changing Love

Your eyes
Seem so small,
There's no spark:
The spark that set fire to the buildings
Of distress within me
As they met mine.

Your face
Seems so ordinary,
So pale as if the blood has been drained –
Sucked dry.

Your lips
Seem so unreal
Because I cannot
Recall the touch of them,
Cannot remember
Their softness anymore.

Your hair
Doesn't seem to
Invite me to ruffle it,
To play with it.

My eyes are the same
That see you, I'm sure.
Is it my love for you
That is changing?

Another Woman's Poem

Forget about the way
His face moved, in vain
Or in sanity,
Or the way his words,
Came out of his mouth
Like dragon's fire.
Or how his hands
Like waves, both
Pleasant and destructive,
Made me feel
From time-to-time.

Forget about everything
Substantial,
Just his name
On my screen
In another woman's poem
Burns me even today –
Just like a callous child
Who turns on the stove
And forgets to light it,
Setting his mother who clicks
The lighter, on fire.

I'm sure
He must be something.

Cry

Some nights you will cry harder
Than all the times before,
It'd be quiet
With the sobs echoing
But let yourself cry, darling.
Those are the tears that
Turn into magic and miracles.
Don't we all know we are weak?
Why lose direction,
Pretend to be strong?
Let yourself cry,
Cry as hard as you can.
Forget about how the pain began.

These tears will dry,
Healing your bruises,
Filling up the voids,
So that after the mourning,
You sleep and wake up
To a beautiful morning.

Bare Shoulder

I wore my disloyalty
As my favourite stole
Because it was too cold
For my skin to be true.

But that bloody stole
Kept slipping
Over and over
From my bare shoulder.

Strings

I wish I were naive
Like a new-born
Despite their experience of pain
At the menacing sound of scissors
That cut the only cord
With their mother
But lets it go anyway.
Together, it's such a surreal bond,
Falling apart.
Fact at one end,
At the other – fantasy.

Growing up
Is like creating
Invisible umbilical cords,
Pulling them
And being pulled by them
Over and over.
Every single time
One breaks, it feels like
Everything else is breaking too,
With someone to hold me sometimes
And sometimes not.

Layers of Soot

Sigh.
Kiss.

Our love was
A simple breathing barter,
Don't know
When and how
The polluted air
Choked
The love away.

Now there are only layers of soot
Between my inhale and your exhale.

Come Soon, You

Come soon, you.
The evening feels so hollow
Without you.

Come soon, you.
I want to dive in
But the heart is shallow,
I always end up hurting my head
When I dive deep into the water.

Come soon, you.
I want an ocean to swim in –
Salty and flirtatious
But also giving, tender,
Transparent and endless.

Come soon, you.
Take away my obsessions
And become my trip in a hot box.
Become my travel,
Unravel me
Like an old sweater
Your grandma made for your father –
One that fits you just fine.
Unravel me, thread by thread,
Wreck me, brick by brick.
There are no shortcuts here,

No cheat codes, no bribes.
It would be painful,
But unravel me anyway,
Wreck me anyway.

Come soon, you.
Let's make sand castles
Only to watch them dissolve at the crack of dawn.
Let's click selfies –
Tell me that I am dark and you are fairer than me.
Let's fight about racism, casteism, sexism, feminism
And why there's no such thing as masculism.

Let's fight to be with another
And then make it up to each other,
Licking the melting bar of Galaxy
In our own Milky Way,
Counting the same stars,
Every night
Under the starry ceiling
Painted fluorescent,
Even then, getting two different numbers,
But I will lie for you and let you win, I swear.
So just come,
Come soon, you.

Invite

I invite
Everyone home,
Hoping that they would fill
The voids you created
With the fire on your finger tips
Like a lit cigarette,
Engraving love onto me.

The well you dug
With your bare tongue
Inside me,
I quench it
With sly connotations,
Smelling the tobacco
On my index finger,
Conversations that traverse,
Strong coffee
Changing playlists
Poetry
Cloudy skies
Windows and windy evenings;
I calm it with rationale.

I bind myself
Into schedules
Of do's and don'ts
And irrational, compulsive behaviour.

The iPhone with its
Recently deleted images –
I can't press delete, twice.

I don't know what they were thinking.

Rooms That I Built

Wandering within my heart
Tonight, there are explosions
In the rooms that I built,
Designed so perfectly
To fit your fury
And a window
For you to peek
At me, anxiously.

Tonight, there is a fire
On the curtains
I chose for you,
On the wall paint
Mixing with one another.
Such a mess
This little nest – destroyed.

Within my heart,
Wandering,
Tonight, there are explosions
Caused by tiny, unfathomed sparks.

Whorehouse

I have no words tonight,
I had so much to say yesterday.

A burning coil
That destroyed my favourite blanket –
Has that caught me off-guard
With all the loss and pain?
Or was it the wish to go back to those moments
Where he walked into that room
And asked me,
"Was this a whorehouse before?
Why are there lipstick marks all over the wall?"
I chuckled at his amusement.

I could look right into his eyes and not be afraid.
He sat next to me,
And kissed me
Told me how much he wanted me
Without any words.

He had no words for me then,
I have no words for him now.

Paranoia Is Contagious

I'm living your fear.
It's funny that paranoia is contagious.
Insecurity weaving its web
Like spiders
Everywhere, until one fine day
Someone decides to clear the mess.

But it takes
Time, hours, days
Sometimes weeks,
A lot of energy,
And patience –
I lack all of it, love.

I miss us, do you?
You confuse me
With the way you try to push me away.
Why?

A little bit of my heart at a time,
Scooping it out –
Your favourite ice cream,
It's melting,
Dripping onto your clothes.
Will you ever
Get rid of these stains?

I live your fear, tonight.
Every night.

Sadness is a communicable disease –
Sometimes incurable,
Horribly painful.

Resume already,
Longer pauses between
Your sweet tunes
Make me feel like the music is over.
Is it?

Dusky, Disloyal Skin

Blurred colours
Of street lights
And the passing trucks
Remind me of blurred memories
That I have of your soft hands
Caressing my body,
Demanding more
And more
Of the dusky, disloyal skin
Crafted with imperfection.
Flowing within,
My love for you.

The reflection of the
Sign boards and
Hoardings
On the wet roads
Just as the rain has stopped
Pulls me back
To the brightness in your small room
Where my eyes turn blind to light
From everywhere but your eyes.

These pushes and pulls
Of the rickety bus
Takes me back
To the time
When we were pulled together
By our hearts,
But our conscience pushed us apart.

Constraint in time and space
Reminds me of us, so
Limited in breaths and just four hands...
I hate it when they split up into
Two and two.

Every small road trip
Is like kissing you,
I wonder what a world tour would
Make me feel.

All the Travel

Kashmir

Beauty in its skin and bones,
Terror flows in its veins.
Snow falls from the sky,
Making it white.
Missiles and bombs
Thrown by the men
Making it black
With the ashes
From the burnt wooden houses,
As if Satan's having
A bonfire too often.
Firing from all
Eight directions
Painting it red,
Spilling innocent blood.
They probably call it
Heaven for its
Huge trees
And beautiful scenery
Or maybe because
It has all the colours –
Red, blue, brown
And lots of green.
Has anyone realized
Or is it just me who thinks
That wars occur to
Claim power on beauty?

Every war occurs to
Gain access to love.
Every war occurs for
Peace by causing
A hell of misery.

Dhauladhar Range

Covered in a
Blanket of clouds,
Dhauladhar is blushing
Like a young bride
Not ready to show
Her face at this dusk –
She is as white as snow,
With freckles
And sharp finger nails.

She takes her fingers
To curtain her face
But her eyes,
They peek at us.
She puts it back
When we stare
In awe and wonder.

I know she waited
For me to write
A poem about her.
Look at her now,
Showing off
Her beautiful body,
Asking me,
"Where have you been?"

Kerala Buses

When the buses are driven
Like bikes
By drivers with spikes –
Hurried: left and then right,
School girls falling on each other.
The hands and the wheels
Rushed with momentum,
Saved somehow from colliding into
The walls
Along these small roads.

Does Newton's Law
Hold true for this little town?

Tickets of every colour
Flutter across the face
Of the conductor.

Birds sitting on electric wires
Fly at once, loud horns like a gunshot –
Followed by a longer pause.

Bangalore Sky

The Bangalore sky
Is a half-baked
Blueberry cheesecake,
An attempt
By an impatient young boy.

The clouds look so reachable,
Like whipped cream.
He watches the waves of the oven – the sun
Playing around,
Going in circles:
Oblivious to the hot summer
And the cold winter
But only a pinch of flavour
With a dash of vinegar.

It looks so awfully luscious,
I want to grab a piece of it
And take it home.

Boat Song

She blushes, as if
He was her childhood lover,
Lost in his own endeavours.
For years,
Out of reach –
Far, between few phone calls.

No one saw her crack jokes before;
As he sings, she wants an encore.
Their hearts roar in silence:
Beautiful violence.

Was it a love letter that never reached?
Was it the religions that they followed?
Was it society? Was it the Almighty?

Her laughter, like musical progressions:
From a smile to hysteria,
Swaying away his obsessions.

It's rare to see
Two beautiful smiles together,
Smiling at one another.

Mere Observer

I am a mere observer
Of all interpretations
Hypotheses and sciences.

I am a mere spectator
Of all the dust and greenery,
Street lights and birds.

I am a mere audience
Of plays and movies,
Movements and paints.

I am a mere mover
In the stillness of the sun,
Of the trees that wish
To touch the sky.

I am a mere worshipper
Of bricks, edges and wounds:
Phony and mundane.

I am a mere mortal
Not safe from death
And dengue, guns, syringes.

I am a mere lover
Of the loved, admired,
Hidden, escaped and terrible.

I am a mere keeper
Of the torn post cards, soft toys,
Tissue papers and chapped lips.

I am a mere dancer
At the little ceremonies and weddings
Of anger, pain, sorrow.

I am a mere traveller
Under the sunsets and the skies,
Searching for fireflies.

I am a woman
Of the man-made world,
Decorated with puns.

Fort Kochi

Running in the rains,
Catching boats to places –
Seriously,
Am I dreaming?
It's like one step here
And another
In a parallel universe.

So serene –
Some things
Like these
Can only be experienced,
One would say –
Rarely can be captured
In photographs or words.

A 40-Hour Train Ride

My nose and hands, freezing
While I put my feet under the brown blanket,
Shutting myself from the world
In the side, upper berth
Of a train that's taking me home.
I made it dark,
Then I adjusted my curtains
To let a little light.
Come into my coupe
So that I can read
The neglected words
Of Gulzar.
I cannot talk today,
Because my throat hurts –
I can barely whisper my name
But I listen to Pink Floyd's
Coming Back to Life
As I start to forget my own voice.
It reminds me of a shell
I used to live in: self-created,
Shutting everyone out
Letting a little light enter me
Through the cracks
That were made by the ones I loved.

Acrimonious

Acrimonious patterns
Of the incongruous noises
That vehicles make outside my window;
The water keeps dripping
From a tap that refused to shut.

A plant I got during happier times
Is dead and wilted
Just like this small town –
I don't water it anymore.
I never watered it anyway.
Such a disgrace to sunshine
And no respect for life.

I see a teen riding the same bike
That he had when we were younger,
Reading sign boards.
On the road, he is smiling
Trying to hide his anxiety,
Denying he has lost his way –
In this moment, he makes me miss him.

I often wonder why fairy lights break so easily.
I wonder why my favourite top fades when I wash it,
Ruining all the other clothes in the bucket.
I often wonder how to be so careful
About every little thing,

About the plant that died
And the top that faded and dried
While everyone is just throwing
"I do not care"
In the air
For everything.

I often miss
How our heartbeats created a melody
Amidst all this
Discordant cacophony.

Shikara

In this *shikara* of life,
I'm trying to balance
All the emotions
Over this buoy,
Saving myself from sinking.

The wind is restless,
Just like my heart,
Caressing, yet chaotic –
Of messy hair and flowing kaftans.

The sun, always so bright,
Sparkling like a short circuit
In these backwaters,
That were left behind.
Making seductive patterns
As I scribble down this poem,
Hoping to see the ocean,
Hoping to touch the horizon.
A million diamonds
Emerge on the surface,
So near, yet so unreachable.
Are they even real
Or just another illusion?

She wonders, as I do too.
Does the sea even exist
Or eternal love
Just another delusion?

Home Is an Elusive Idea

Home is an elusive idea,
Just out of reach forever.

Packing bags for another affair;
If home is where the heart is,
I sure am broken-hearted
With pieces of my heart
Shattered and flying
In all directions:
The one I grew up in,
One where my parents stay,
A home that I've known not of
And is very far away.

Hanging family photographs
And random doodles on the walls,
Taking them down every time I leave
Is the only goodbye gift –
Almost like a detached love note.

Affection for trees outside the window,
Unspoken, unexplained...
Lived in so many random rooms till now,
Leaving a part of me there.

I attempt to pack my entire life
Into bags and load them into trucks
But I always fail to grasp
The whole of my heart.

I think I am where I've stayed,
I am those who smiled or stared
And those who really cared.
I am what I ate and drank,
I am the pages of old notebooks
Both filled and blank.
I am the autos and buses I travelled in,
I am those that drove them too.
Look at me, it's true.
Every time I move to a new place,
I expose, I exclude, not demean and erase
All at once, what I have been.

I am crying for all the homes,
Striving for all the pieces of my heart
That flew like papers in the wind,
Like ashes, from the death of the old –
Unless my heart is brought back to one,
Wanderlust is the only hope of healing.

Constellations

As I lead my life
Laying on the terrace floor,
Talking to silver stars
With their divine being,
Tonight, I see constellations.

Yellows on the right,
Reds on the left
Of the headlights of trucks and cars
Being driven home
From above, as I
Fly back home too.

Beauty is not in squares and angles,
It's in havoc and chaos.
The truth of life is
There are as many stars
On land as in the sky.
There is only as much goodness
In you, as you discern in others.
There are aesthetics outside
Only as much as within you.

As the solid blue
Fades into orange,
The sun is setting
And rising for someone else.

In the world, there's always day
And there's always night,
And there is shimmering white.

Inevitably,
You shall find it,
Whatever you seek.

Indian Traffic Jam

Love of a broken heart
Is like an Indian traffic jam,
Always trying to
Squeeze into the little gaps on the road
With rage
With obsession
With impatience;
In a hurry
To go back to the lover.

There are voids to fill,
Caulk all cracks.
However, the red lights of the signals
And the thought police,
The zebra crossings of infatuation –
That does not matter.

There is pollution
From the last vehicle of love.
The one ahead
Chokes you –
Causes haziness,
For the broken heart
Is young and carefree.
Breaking bones,
Chipping teeth
In the accidents of mad love.

Seeking the lost shards
That puncture tyres
For no reason.

There are fines to be paid
All so vulnerable without helmets,
Causing hurt and misery
If it may.

So needy to be
Out of this way,
But falling back into it
Again and again.
More and more.
Deeper and deeper.

All That in Between

Abuse

Since humanity began to evolve,
It has been deteriorating –
Less
Lesser
Lesser with time.

Just like a million other people,
She too was once
Reduced
Abused,
With words, with sex,
With corruption;
"What?"
Our hypocritical society – perplexed
At the mention of it,
Because they are blindfolded...
Deaf when a little girl screams
And attempts suicide
Because of that
One
Bad
Touch.

It's funny how serious issues have such light terms –

Bad
Touch.

Denial – displacing it
Passing it on
Again and again,
Full of recrimination
And hatred –
Wearing only a mask
Of innocence
That was once stripped away
Inside a washroom...
Pulled by the arm,
Forced,
Piece by piece,
Cloth by cloth
Till every inch of naivety
Was washed away
With the naked bodies
Under the tap.

Now, vengeful enough,
She roams around till she hunts down
And leaves
Anyone who dares to love her
Barely feeling anything anymore –
Her soul still unsatisfied.

Can a severe childhood trauma
Be erased
By several little traumas
Caused to others?

Last Words

In my head,
I'm repeating your last words
And the one before
And the one before that.
In my head,
I'm wishing that there was
Something I could have said
That would have mended things,
That would've shaken your insides,
Sent chills down your spine.
In my head,
I'm repeating
What you said
When I had my head
On your lap
And I thought,
"This is it!"
You were finally here
To comfort the little things
That fuck with my mind
Once in a while.
You were here to listen,
You let me scream till I felt alright.
In my head,
I am repeating what you said.

Grey Talks

Vague endings to heavy conversations
Feel like a cold hug during passionate love-making
Sweat turns to glaciers in a moment.
Screaming in the vacuum,
The sound of our voices cannot be heard anymore.
So easy to burst and drop on the floor.

The vapour of love: omnipresent,
So does the sun sway?
But then, why don't rainbows always stay?
Do they need more tears, heavier rains?

Soaked, dripping emotions,
Sucked, hollow at once,
The silences are dark corridors –
All of us locked behind different doors,
Reaching out with hope,
Watching the same blue sky,
Whispered, unheard, empty cries,
Caressing the naked tips of our fingers
To be swallowed back again.

Do I cease to exist if someone ceases to perceive me?

Floating Stars

Floating stars
Distant in the sea,
Almost near the horizon.

Twinkling ships
Sailing in the sky,
Looking for lighthouses.

All of them
Trying to make
Their way
Back to their homes.

Longing.

Same Old Road

Same old road,
Same old rag,
The edges of the steel bowl,
Rusted and cracked.
What does she seek?

A good meal,
An honest smile
Once in a while,
Or a conversation
About the weather,
Or maybe about how weak
She feels…
The sadness on her cheek,
Is it the losing streak?
Of what does she speak?

A baby wailing
At the top of its voice,
Lying on her right thigh,
Shifting and turning,
There's no comforting silk
Or barely any milk to feed,
No books to read,
No Band-Aid for when she bleeds.
What does she plead?

A few words of kindness
And light to her blindness,
Begging to be freed.
What does she need?

Same old road
Under the same old tree.

Things

Little things.
Listening to old voice notes,
Catching up with an old friend,
Finding an old picture,
Being grateful
For blissful beaches,
Lush, green pathways;
A splendid mix
Of the old and the new
In it and through.
Little things,
Like I said.

Little things.

The Fans Are Angry Tonight

The fans are angry tonight –
The windows are creaking behind.
My phone's on loud,
Singing the chorus
Of *Silence of My Mind*.

Trumpets and saxophones,
Flutes and violins,
Shifting
From harmony to violence
Through my headphones,
Playing around with my sleep.

"Should I weep?" I ask.
Or should I wait?
And then, suddenly,
There's no anger
As I think to myself,
The fairies light up, pink.
I'd go to sleep
When I run out of ink.

"Should I be asleep?" I ask.
Or should I write?
It's too late tonight.
It is late, tonight.

Ruffle Like a Rose

I have not known
How not to be in love,
Like a foodie who never knew
How not to be hungry.

I have not known
How to not be
So mad, so obsessed, so sad
About something.

Someone says or does
Or just looks up
But not to look at me;
Waves his hand
But not at me.
So if someone goes around
Claiming to be in love
I chuckle;
I ruffle
Like a rose that was never preserved
In a Jane Austen novel.

I have not known at all
How not to love,
How not to think of someone

Before I sleep
Every night.
Like a compulsive ritual in a temple
That a priest has to perform right –
Maybe because he knows no other way.

I wonder what people think of
When they are not in love,
When they are not moved
By little things.
How do they make sense
Of my poetry
Or anyone else's?

Two Cups of Tea

Two cups of tea,
You and me.
What's lovelier?
A drive so long
And all the songs
We love.

Watching Me

I laughed so hard today
That I fell on the ground.
Ma was watching me,
She was laughing too.
She says she can see
Through me
And I wonder if she
Sees you too
In my sorrow, in my anguish,
In that fraction of a second
Of the break I take
Between choking laughter
When I pause to breathe
And you come rushing in
Filling in the minute spaces
Of my sponge-like mind,
Like water.

The way air gets sucked into vacuum
Through a tiny hole
Is how I truly miss you.
Between two breaths
Between the laughter
Between the space
Where two colours merge
On my palette.

Diwali

In the hope
That every little evil
Within us will burn,
We burst and burn
The crackers outside.
Is the smoke I see
Your jealousy parting?
Is the noise of the crackers
All the screams you suppressed
And the laughter that came out right?
The dogs are barking too much
This *Diwali* too,
As if they can see
The ghosts coming out to dance
And welcoming the Gods;
The best of decorations brought
To entrances of these houses
Showing off their best clothes,
And even better smiles.

There are children on the streets
So happy,
Playing with explosives,
Welcoming inflammatory youth.
Oh! So many colours in the sky,
They make me blink too much.

I see *diyas* –
The flames: curving and flickering.
The light doesn't die...
We are all struggling
To wish each other by all means
So the love doesn't die.

That Kid

I think I am
Still that kid
Who loves herself
When someone else loves her;
Who feels awful
When someone stops caring enough.

What a terrible life I lead,
Still being a child
In this world full of adults
With their games of hide & seek.

Bad Cat

The cat's eyes,
Cute and witty –
They never cry.
Cunning love
Have you ever seen
The way a cat walks?
Ailurophiles that we are,
Envying the green eyes
Shining in the night,
Hiding its plight.
I wonder if the wolves turn,
Looking at them gleam
Confusing it with moonlight.

Then again,
There is the murmuring
As the cat crosses the road,
"Oh, it's black."
As if it's dipped in ink
Dripping black along its way
Swaying the bad, bad luck.

Countless Nights

I have seen
Countless nights
Turn into mornings,
Drinking water,
Listening to the same playlists
Perhaps for the 87th time;
On the seventh floor,
Enjoying the show
Of eagles at dawn
As if the sky were a circus.
There is mist, the sun's barely there;
Coconut trees, so tall,
Yet below me,
Covering the sight
Of the roads and poverty.
I can see the sea
Peeping out of the horizon
Camouflaged with grey lines.

Wearing my usual blue and green,
I wait for the day to arrive
For me to pass out
Amidst the texts: vibrating
And the loud horns.

Old Monk

The night we meet
I will make you a drink
Of my poetry
And water
Just like your Old Monk,
Get you drunk
And maybe then
You would know
How I feel
When I act crazy.
Gulp it down slowly, love,
Sip by sip,
No shots, no bottoms up
'Cause it's hard to handle
Two crazy people at a time.
And when you are wasted enough,
You would probably understand this rhyme.

Indian Cricket

Kill me for this if you have to.
Just wondering
How little things
Like "last seen" and blue tick marks,
A game of a bat and a ball –
50 overs and 9 wickets
Affect people around me.
Kill me for this if you have to.
Just wondering what you will get
Out of my death if you do.

Just like drops
Of water on a hot pan,
Little things
Can burn us and leave scars –
Both internal and external,
If we are too heated up in life.

Existential Crisis

Grocery Lists

Grocery lists
And things to do,
Timetables and schedules –
These are socially acceptable
Remedies for anxiety
That silence brings.

But once in a while
When you are walking alone
On an empty street,
It starts drizzling
And it's too hard to manage
An umbrella and a bag
And the fear of spoiling
Your not-so-smartphone.

Don't you feel like throwing it all away,
Spreading your arms,
Facing the sky
And realizing
That it's not even raining hard?
It should be pouring,
Clearing all that we hold
In those little structures we make,
In the meetings we hold
And the speeches we prepare;
We always forget to say

The simple things
That matter.

I envy the coconut trees
Keeping their heads high
Enjoying the rain fearlessly...
Ambitiously rather,
Like this is all there is
To the life they preach,
And yet being more useful to the world
Than most of us will ever be.

Who are we really fooling?

In My Superman Pyjamas

In my Superman pyjamas –
Lying on this wooden bench,
My legs in the air
And my hair on the ground.
I write these words
With pure honesty –
Give a little love, it plays,
My ears plugged.
Give a little love, it says,
My heart shrugged
Contemplating about all the ifs.
Do these words mean
Anything to anyone?
Do these words come
Like just another
Poem, read and praised
But abandoned in distaste?
Does anyone at all
Hug these words
Some nights
As they struggle to fall asleep
When a pillow
Is just not enough?
Do they? Do you? Do I?

Home

Where I can be
Irresponsible and cared for,
Home is plain laughter
At the jokes on each other,
Mostly the mother.
Early morning *poha* or *parantha*
As my dogs – Star and Shine
Try to wake me up,
But I force myself to sleep
On a bed that comforts me
In my heartbreak;
I pressed myself hard against it
When I wanted to hold someone.
Home is eating and praying,
Mutual obsession and self-love;
Home is TV and Wi-Fi
No accounts for petrol or pot.
When I know someone is waiting for me
With a meal to feed my heart,
The stomach stays full every day anyway.
Home is a phone call
From my mum, saying,
"Come home now,
You've been out all day!"

Two Lines

Two lines came hand-in-hand, you know
And knocked on my door,
I was busy on Facebook, I won't lie
And missed the doorbell.

Two lines were laughing, singing, you know
And calling my name,
I was busy reading others' lines, I won't lie
And missed their sweet voices.

Two lines were playing see-saw, you know
And jumping around the swings outside,
I was busy lazing, I won't lie
And missed playing with them.

Two lines giggled at my door, you know –
One a little fat, the other a little more.
I was busy feeding myself then, I won't lie
And missed sharing a meal with them.

Two lines: I watched them go,
Hands around each other's backs
And legs in synchrony,
Leaving this feeling of a forgotten poem
Even before I had begun writing it.

Just in Time

She was not my mother
But no less;
In that moment,
As I looked at her
From the corner of my eye
Falling at ends,
And my lips: trembling,
With no words to say
Even though I knew it all.
She said "Own up,
You know the answers,
Tell them what you know"
I tried, slowly,
And in the back of my head,
I could only think
About when I sink,
And I find a person
Who could tell me
That I can cross rough rivers easily.
If only
When I look up,
I have someone looking at me
In that same moment.

Love Exchange

If I could exchange you
For poetry,
You'd cost me all the words
I have ever said
Or even thought of –
Your lips, your eyes and your ears
In exchange for couplets,
Your breath on my neck for rhymes
Your kiss would cost me a library
Your touch, an entire lifetime.

For every poem,
A moment with you I'd trade,
A pinch of metaphors I'd drop in your tea
For all the eye contact you made.
I'd hold your hand and tell you
That I can't write sonnets
But I will write of your laughter,
Your sorrow, your anger, your regrets.

With every "I love you" you say
I'd quote Plath, Poe and Williams Carlos Williams –
Speechless,
Despite innumerable whiskey sours and whatever rum.

If ever you sleep next to me,
I'd paint my dreams in poetry;
I could barter the imagination
That flows through my veins,
If you pour a cup of tea for me,
I'd add cubes of similes
For all the words you ever say to me.
Your love would suck the poet out of me
If I could exchange you for poetry.

A peck on my forehead
Could wipe off the writer's block
Like my knotted nerves – relaxed again.
If you ever cry, I'd take all your misery away
And give you all the poems
Scribbled on the back of my notebooks
Written on those dull days during boring lectures,
About that one look of yours.

As I leave, I'd hand you over
All the half-burnt, torn and folded sheets
Of silliness I poured out from my heart,
With a post-it barely stuck on it,
Saying

Yours truly.

P.S., it would say,
I would never know how else to love you
But through words,
So I'd rather have you in my poems,
You never loved me anyway.

Yours truly.

New Year

This is the end of another year
And sometimes one end
Feels like the end of everything.
The year is going away,
Dying rather,
Because it is never coming back.
Some part of me
Is going to die again,
Some part of me
Will be erased
With resolutions I make to fool myself
But the last day feels
Like the last of all misery.

What's really going to change
Apart from a number
On the top right corner
Of our notebooks?
Maybe the next morning might
Bring sunshine that's more yellow
And butterflies more colourful
But if we notice closely,
Every tomorrow of our lives
Gets a little better than yesterday.
Only if we notice closely.

Imaginary Hellos

Longing for a "Hello"
It's always been incomplete,
Meaningless conversations;
Such hollow bones.
It's 1:00 in the morning,
My eyes hurt but I'm staring at the blank spaces
Filled with unreal hellos from you,
Without ever having to say goodbye.

Blue Tick Marks

I'm demeaning others
Like the others are demeaning me;
I don't pick up calls, messages I do not see,
I laugh about emails I receive,
I do not read.
I complain about blue tick marks and "last seen"
And late at night,
Amidst chocolate cookies and green tea,
I tell a friend about a man I dream of.
I scream about the void,
Shut my ears to my own noise –
Such havoc of loneliness and a busy life,
Swinging and hanging loose.
I need my sleep and I need my muse,
I do not know if I am ready
To invest my words in someone else again.
I do not know if I will ever be.

Oh, Bride

"Oh, bride! Get ready, it's time.
Fix your *bindi*,
Wipe the smudged mascara.
Smile subtly.
It's time."
"But, mother, my arms hurt
Six yards of cloth is hard to handle."
"How a woman handles her saree
Defines her for life.
Oh, bride! Don't peep out of the window.
It's time."
"Flowers in my head can't be seen,
Mother, what does this *purdah* mean?"

"I have been there too, bride.
Your sister, your grandma, your aunt,
We all have been there."
"But..."
"Bride, be polite and calm."
The *pallu* of her mother's saree
Neatly dabs the tears,
Wiping away all her hopes and fears.
"Come! It's time."

Poems That Die

There are so many poems
That die inside me every day
Just like:
The fallen, ripe fruits that were not eaten – decomposing.
Hundreds of eggs and millions of sperms that never see life.
A sweater that a grandmother knits
But never could finish.
A dying river that cannot make it to the ocean.
A soldier who loses his life winning the battle.
There are so many poems that die inside me
Every single day.

Outside the Box

I have always wondered
If we had to think
Outside the box;
Who the fuck created this box anyway?

The rains were meant to be felt
On the skin,
Meant to be soaked in,
So who made the shed
An umbrella anyway?

Sunshine is awful,
Let there be dark clouds with silver linings,
That we're supposed to take in
With our naked eyes;
Sunglasses –
Whose idea was it anyway?

Just because we have options
Like divorce, break-up,
Causing heartache,
We have forgotten
How to truly love,
How to feel
Terrible about each other
And then cuddle anyway.

We humans,
We like to save dogs
Because they are adorable,
And kill chickens, goats and cows
Buffaloes, crabs, prawns and what not.
What bullshit!
Who created the food chain anyway?

Touch

Until someone touches you,
It's all just skin and bones.
Only later, the adrenaline
And oxytocin was truly felt.
You learn about your body
Only when the hand
Goes down the curves
Of your mortal body.
It is fortunate, yet so unfortunate
That someone
Else defines it.
Until then,
It just exists
Without any acknowledgement or definition.

An act of touch
Performs subtle wonders,
Like little magic tricks of childhood.

Time Warp

Have you seen the halo around the moon?
Like the morning milk that curdles by afternoon
Or like the word that comes out from a careless mouth so
    soon;
Have you seen the halo around the moon?

Tonight, we laugh like children –
For there is no time and space for them.
They run and fall and bruise themselves,
They dream as their mother feeds them.
Darkness is not bad at all.
It is, thus, only a childhood fear of disparity,
Who wants a floating world when we have got gravity?
That's exactly when the imaginations grow,
I sigh, and you sigh, at the wilderness and flow.
What if we all were the same person,
Interacting with one another like the cells of the same body,
Living in different times and centuries?
Would we still behave the same with each other?

Loosened associations

Forget about technology
And wait for the train
'Cause when it comes
It will arrive like the rain
On a dry day.
Tempting Subway
Dizzy eyes
Silky chocolate
A little fruity and
A whole lotta nutty –
Just like life.

Nostalgia makes me nauseous;
Throwbacks lead to throw-ups,
Burnt hair and tarred lungs.

And a good night.

Destination

I was looking for someone
I could travel this long way with;
I was trying to find
Where I belonged,
And somewhere between the chaos
Across these roads,
You became my destination.

Silhouettes

All these countless stories
Are just silhouettes
To what goes around in the universe –
Infinite solar systems,
And billions of planets
Revolving around a mediocre star
In their own classical ways: set patterns.

These stories are filled with
Little details,
Heart breaks,
Chipped nails,
Thousands of genres – harmonizing,
Fair and dark skin,
So many prayers to so many Gods
Castes, creeds and races,
Drawing lines,
Creating political parties,
Building boundaries,
Even when the sunlight remains the same.

The concept of time and space
Is delusional;
What if everyone around us
Is merely a part of our imagination?
A part of our own fears, wishes and desires.

What if life was just a dream?
And death, the true state of consciousness;
Perhaps, dying is an act of waking up.
And you'd die with me, as I would too, one day.
All the silhouettes
And shadows
Will be sucked in,
Colliding and collapsing
Into just one soul –
My soul.
Because what I see around me
Is nothing but a part of me.

It's nothing, but a dream
With a definite beginning
And an end, natural or unnatural,
But both ending with cries.

Dead Baby Comes Alive

Kohl-lined eyes, black tears,
Afraid with so many fears;
They say
Dead baby comes alive
Out of danger: confide.

Dingy garage and a degree
Detangled dangerously;
They say
Dead baby comes alive.

Bordering on the absurd,
Shrill cries: weird.
The ghosts of Venice
Destroy the poetry of the place.
Where to hide?
The night is dark, the days are darker,
Hammering, shattering thy skull from within.
Dead?

No angel, but the devil in disguise –
Disabled & discouraged,
Harder than a maze.

God foresees trouble,
Screams louder, dangles double;
Keep in mind the reasons,

Deliver inflammatory voices, no guns.
Black tears are not dry,
Can you not see the burns?

The Almighty replied,
"Try harmony, bullets were always naive
Oh! And the dead baby never did die!"

Seasons

Winters I

Winter sure is a cold woman –
She finds a man to keep her warm.
She's lazy
Wakes up late
Does not prepare tea
But yawns throughout the day.

She blurs things with fog,
Keeps her feet from getting cold
By petting her dog;
She sure is a cold, cold woman
But she brings Christmas with her,
To make it up, lets the little children
Come out and decorate the tree
With beautiful things.
She is kind sometimes –
Let's the sun take half-days at work,
She has a kind of smirk
That no season would ever understand.
She's a brat
And sets the sky just right
That the stars
Become the shiny sequence
On her pretty scarf.

She's neurotic –
The fingers and feet get hurt

At the slightest of touch,
But there are holidays for everyone
Enough to take naps anytime during the day.

When I look at her
After four long years
She smiles at me
Because only she knows
What she just did with my poetry.

Winters II

So many jitters
That bitter love has given,
Hardly any warmth
To calm this cold weather;
Of all the breaths he ever took,
I always wished he would inhale me
Like his favourite fragrance
But my fingers were left aloof
Like my heart
For so long,
Turning pale;
That winter had become
My favourite season.
Someone rushed in
Like warm sunlight on a freezing day
And now, I've almost forgotten
What winters feel like against my skin,
But I won't lie and admit
My heart has a vague memory of it,

Sometimes it plays bluff
When the warmth is scarce

Raindrops on My Umbrella

I love the sound
Of raindrops on my umbrella,
I feel safe yet at risk
At the same time.
It reminds me of you –
Makes me nostalgic
Of the time when you seemed so far...
Untouchable, at a distance
Despite being near.

This attempt of breaking the umbrella
Feels like the moments when you tried
To break through my walls
And said, "Show me where it hurts
Let me heal you."
I check the wind
And the direction of the rain,
Put my hand out only to get a little wet.
I use a borrowed purple umbrella
To keep myself from getting drenched.
This reminds me of you.
All of this.

But, love,
I get drenched anyway.
You know your way in

Just like the rains –
Multiple
Innovative
And sly.

Sigh.

Slipped

I slipped myself
Under the lush, green quilt
I yawned
As the mountains
Spoilt me
With all their love.

Tragedies

Burning houses of tragedies,
Of course, so painful;
For something new to begin,
We need to clear the ground
Burn the weed,
Level the soil,
Of course, so painful.

But, darling,
Beautiful things
Follow the terrible;
Summers, rains and lush green forests.

Reconstruction comes after
A lot of crying and loss.
Oh, so painful.

Wait.
Let it come.
Evoke it in your
Prayers and daydreams.

Fall

This sunset is like our romance,
Turning the cheeks of the earth pink
Just as it does to mine.
The sun, peeking from the horizon
Before it sets...
An endless ocean of distance below
And the countless clouds above –
That line in between the struggles
Is where you have the last look at me, I know;
A body in the gloomy dusk and the light drizzle.

The earth's rough skin looks the most beautiful
When the sun is just about to leave,
Seducing it one last time,
Trying hard to make it stay;
I often wonder
How crazy a woman she must be,
Revolving, rotating
All day, all night long
To get a little closer
To the man of her dreams.

And tonight, I am hopeful
For both her and myself
That you shall return
From the other side of the world

With the sun and illuminate it all.
We are just two women
Thankful for the stars you left behind
To watch over us.

The Same Blanket

I saw the sky kissing
The terrain of the land –
The way the orange light
Came from the other side between the gaps...

It reminded me of our bodies:
The fire the friction caused
When they rubbed against each other.

It's only the lucky ones that reach the lips,
Others sigh in agony, pain and full of envy.
I saw the best of love meeting and parting
Over and over, yet so beautiful.

Mother Nature
Sleeping in the same blanket as God,
Away from the chaos of the world.

Summer Love

It's wonderful to see
How you and me
Have gotten ourselves
Into this sweet, summer love,
But will it last like the trees?
Or end with autumn like fallen leaves?

You've given me the best of this lifetime,
An altered state of mind, apart from drugs –
Often stronger than the high.
The most sincere, stolen smiles, smirks and grins
And sometimes you chuckled too at the way I whined
About love, about cabs and the dangers of driving fast
While we have rushed
Without worrying for the dangers of life.
"Who holds hands anymore?"
A friend asked me in awe and mockery.
I told him, "I guess... Just us."

Seasons I

We were those lovers;
We are those lovers
Who can never be together,
Just like seasons
That long to meet one another.

One waits
And when the other comes,
The former fades away;
We were those
We are those
We will be those lovers.
Our destinies depend
On each other.

Summer's ruthlessness on earth
Followed by the rain,
Paving the way for Winter;
When lovers go out for a walk,
The girl says, "Oh, such lovely weather!"
The boy agrees, "It couldn't be better."
People talk about it,
Saying there is no heat and
There is no dirt from the rain –
That is when it is the end of my pain.
And the seasons meet,
We meet.

Oh! Such a beauty my love is,
I have it,
And then again, I will never have it.
We wait like seasons...
Wait for one another.

Seasons II

There was a time when
The day had both the rain and the sun;
There was a time when
The night had both stars and storms.
There came a time when the rains dried up
And the storm was calmed by the stars' charm.

Rain, scared of abandonment,
Left the day.
Storm thought the stars were better
Off without her.

And now they hardly meet,
But once in a while
When they meet,
The rain and the sun –
The dull white
Turns into seven colours with joy,
Making my heart rejoice.
And when they meet,
The storm and the stars,
And the dark night sky
Bursts out in thunder and lightning,
Making the sky beautiful.

Seasons III

Love is that summer's sour mango
I won't ever say no to.
That's what it comes down to:
The sleeplessness I always embrace.
That red lace of the cards and letters I love to write,
That orange ink looks so bright
On the blue sky that I want to fill
With scribbles of your name.

It's a game, baby,
It's a game of getting lost that I love to play.
I lose at it every autumn's day and night.
But that smile I get
After you win over and over is my prize.
Judgments pass through me –
I sense deviance in my soul

I long for winters
When every single hurt is so intense,
When every single tear is colder than the other,
When the heart is frozen.
But even then, one touch of yours,
Full of warmth, melts me.

That warmth I trace,
That is when all the love flows –

From my heart to my body like a hot rush,
And I look at you, I blush.

Spring arrives
When I look into your eyes.

Seasons IV

The branch of a tree that I am
You are the flower that makes me beautiful.

You bloom,
And every time you bloom, you fall off of me
And I let you go as you fall to the ground.

And I see a woman carefully picking you up,
Weaving you into her hair.

The still lake that I am,
Forever trapped in the same place –
You grow as a lotus in that dirt that is my heart
To make me beautiful.
You bloom.
And every time you bloom,
You are not mine anymore.
I see a man pluck you for his love
And all I am left with is the fragrance
That lingers from your presence.

You belong with me
And then again,
You will never belong with me.
You bloom.
And you disappear.

Autumn awes me with these words
"He will come again
When the time is right"
Winter smirks at me,
"But he will never stay."
Summer wisely says
"Never abandon him,
That's what makes you beautiful"

Seasons V

What have I been but the wind
To your tree-like soul?
I pass by
And as you wave,
Some leaves fall out of acknowledgement
And the rest out of guilt
Of the failure to love me the way I do you.

Sometimes the wind moves on the beat...
You smile as you bloom.
Sometimes the wind comes with disappointments,
Endless attempts to eliminate your presence.
But the stupid wind,
The foolish me
Fails to understand
That my existence comes hand-in-hand
With that of the tree,
With yours.
No one can see the wind
But only feel as the tree dances with it
Like a flamenco duet.
Why is it that the wind and the trees

Are looked at wrong as they meet?
Isn't their romance as pure as ours?
As awful as our consequences:
All the leaves have dried,

The tree, lonely,
The Wind regresses too,
As they drift apart.

After all, your condition is my fault;
It's the fault of the wind
Letting the tree lose its ornaments
For those few moments.

If there is a time and space,
A season and a weather
For everything,
Then the share of my wind and your tree is too less.

The wind envies the birds
Who build their nests on that tree,
The wind cries over the flowers
That get to be a part of the tree.

What have I been but the wind
To your tree-like soul?
I pass by
And as you wave,
Some leaves fall out of acknowledgement
And the rest out of guilt
Of the failure to love me the way I do you.

Sometimes softly,
Sometimes swift like a hurricane,
I will always come back.

Sometimes cold,
Sometimes a warm breeze,
I will always come back.

I know you will always rustle
Like you are trying to say something in return.

Sometimes a howl,
Sometimes a cry,
I will always come back.

Sometimes a roar,
Sometimes laughter
I will always come back.

What have I been but the wind
To your tree-like soul?

Printed in the United States
By Bookmasters